MW00987479

DOG LADY
AND
THE CUBAN
SWIMMER

TWO ONE-ACT PLAYS
BY MILCHA SANCHEZ-SCOTT

★

★

DRAMATISTS
PLAY SERVICE
INC.

DOG LADY and THE CUBAN SWIMMER
Copyright © 1988, Milcha Sanchez-Scott (Acting Edition)
Copyright © 1984, Milcha Sanchez-Scott

All Rights Reserved

SPECIAL NOTE

ABOUT THE AUTHOR

Milcha Sanchez-Scott's first play, *Latina*, was premiered by L.A. Theatre Works in 1980 and received seven *Drama-Logue* awards. *Dog Lady* and *The Cuban Swimmer* were written during the next two years and were developed as a special project of L.A. Theatre Works in 1982. In 1983 Sanchez-Scott won the Vesta award, given each year to a West Coast woman artist, and in 1983–84 she was a member of INTAR's Hispanic Playwrights-in-Residence Laboratory, directed by Maria Irene Fornes. During her New York residency she began work on a full-length play, *Roosters*, and three one-acts under the collective title *City of Angels*.

DOG LADY and THE CUBAN SWIMMER were presented at INTAR (Max Ferra, Artistic Director) in New York City from April 27 – May 27, 1984

Max Ferra directed. Sets were designed by Ming Cho Lee, costumes by Connie Singer, lighting by Anne E. Militello and sound by Paul Garrity. Mime/movement was by Pilar Garcia. The cast was as follows:

DOG LADY

RAPHAEL	Manual Rivera
ORLANDO	Carlos Carrasco
ROSALINDA LUNA	Jeannette Mirabal
MARIÁ PILAR LUNA	Graciela LeCube
LUISA RUIZ	Lillian Hurst
JESSE LUNA	Elizabeth Pena
MRS. AMADOR	Marcella White
PERCUSSIONISTS	Daniel Barrajanos, Arto Tuncboyaci

THE CUBAN SWIMMER

MARGARITA	Jeannette Mirabal
EDUARDO	Carlos Cestero
SIMÓN	Manuel Rivera
AÍDA	Lillian Hurst
ABUELA	Graciela LeCube
MEL MUNSON	Carlos Carrasco
MARY BETH WHITE	Elizabeth Pena
PERCUSSIONISTS	Daniel Barrajanos, Arto Tuncboyaci

DOG LADY and THE CUBAN SWIMMER were subsequently presented at the Gate Theatre in London, England from April 20 – May 16, 1987. Christa van Raalte directed. The design was by Jane Green. In the cast were Sheila Burrell, Joseph Long, Diana Brookes, Helen Keen, Katharina Tana and Christopher Simon.

CONTENTS

DOG LADY

CHARACTERS

RAPHAEL
ORLANDO, the mailman
ROSALINDA LUNA, the runner
MARÍA PILAR LUNA, Rosalinda's mother
JESSE LUNA, Rosalinda's younger sister
LUISA RUIZ, the Dog Lady
MRS. AMADOR, a neighbor

TIME
Summer.

PLACE
Los Angeles: a small barrio off the Hollywood freeway.

DOG LADY

First Day

Early summer morning. The residential section of Castro Street. There is a large sun, and the sunlight has the particular orange hue that indicates the Santa Ana weather condition.

We see two front yards, enclosed by a low stone or cement fence. One yard is very neat, tidy, almost manicured, with a rotating sprinkler watering the green lawn. The other yard is jungle-like, with strange plants in odd places, rubber tires, all kinds of other rubbish, and a sign in front that reads: "CURANDERA--HEALER". Each yard has a mailbox and on the far side of the neat house, there is a jacaranda tree.

Leaning against the fence is Raphael, a dark, brutal-looking young man of eighteen or nineteen. He has smoldering dark eyes. He is wearing a Cuban T-shirt, khaki pants, a dark felt hat. He is staring at the neat house.

RAPHAEL. (*Like music.*)Rosalinda! (*Enter Orlando, the mailman, carrying his bag. Raphael runs away before Orlando can see him.*)

ORLANDO. (*Walking*) Neither rain, nor sleet, nor snow. . . . Says nothing about the heat . . . not one word about the heat. (*He opens the mailbox of the messy yard and rummages through his bags.*) Nada, ni modo, nothing for you, Doña Luisa. (*Reading sign.*) "Curandera . . . healer." (*Shakes his head.*) It **takes** all kinds. (*Rosalinda comes out of the neat house. She is 18 years old, wearing a jogging shorts outfit. She is quite pretty and feminine. She does some warm-up stretches.*) *Hola* Rosalinda, *ay qué* hot! . . . It's a scorcher . . . it's a sauna . . . you could fry eggs on the sidewalk . . . it's so hot that . . . You gonna run? Today?

ROSALINDA. I'm gonna win, Orlando.

ORLANDO. You're gonna die! This heat could affect your brain.

ROSALINDA. (*Getting into starting position.*) I'm going to run around the world. Today Africa, tomorrow India and Saturday . . .

ORLANDO. The Big One.

ROSALINDA. Rome!

ORLANDO. On your mark. Get set. The whole barrio's behind you. . . . Go! (*Rosalinda runs off. Yelling to Rosalinda.*) May all the Angels come down and blow you over the finish line. (*Walking off.*) Wish we had some rain, some sleet, some snow. (*Exit Orlando. The sun moves up a fraction in the sky to indicate passage of time. In front of the neat yard of the Luna family we see María Pilar Luna, Rosalinda's mother, wearing a fresh housedress and apron. She is standing on the newly swept cement path that leads to her front porch. She has a very determined look as her eyes scan the street. The Luna's neighbor, Luisa Ruiz, is slowly making her way through the rubble and rubbish in her front yard. She is dressed in a torn, stained, dingy white bathrobe. Although her lips are painted a bright red, her hair has not been combed. The overall effect is that she looks not unlike her front yard.*)

MARÍA PILAR. Rosalinda! Rosalinda!

LUISA RUIZ. *Buenos días*, María Pilar. It's a beautiful Santa Ana Day, *que no?*

MARÍA PILAR. *Buenos días*, Doña Luisa. *Sí, sí* it's a beautiful day. Rosalinda! *Ay, dónde está, esa muchacha?* Rosalinda!

LUISA RUIZ. Are you looking for Rosalinda?

MARÍA PILAR. No, I'm doing this for the good of my health.

LUISA RUIZ. Oh. Maybe a tea of wild pepper grass.

MARÍA PILAR. I'm only joking, Doña Luisa, I'm already under the doctor's care, thank you.

LUISA RUIZ. Oh. You're welcome.

MARÍA PILAR. Rosalinda! Rosalinda!

LUISA RUIZ. Where is she?

MARÍA PILAR. Ay, Doña Luisa, believe me, if I knew where Rosalinda was, I wouldn't be calling for her. Rosalinda!

LUISA RUIZ. Sometimes if you whistle, they come. El Bobo only comes when I whistle.

MARÍA PILAR. El Bobo?

LUISA RUIZ. The big one. He's a . . . a . . . Labrador retriever. He only comes when I whistle. Once the people complained so I got one of them ultrasonic dog whistles, but when I blow it, Mr. Mura says it opens up his garage door.

MARÍA PILAR. Doña Luisa, my daughter is not a dog to be whistled for.

LUISA RUIZ. Oh. Now El Pepe, he's the cockapoo, they're not so independent, you know. He comes whenever you just call him.

MARÍA PILAR. Rosalinda! (*Holding her stomach.*) Ay, this screaming is making me acid. (*She yells toward the house.*) Jesse! Jesse! Andale, baby, get me the Rolaids. They're on top of *la llelera*. You hear me, Jesse?

LUISA RUIZ. You just say "Pepe, Pepe" and he just comes running, wagging his tail, happy to see you. Not like Esmerelda, she's the collie that stays in the window all the time.

MARÍA PILAR. Jesse! The Rolaids!

JESSE. (*Offstage*) I can't find them, Mom.

MARÍA PILAR. On top of la refrigerator, I said.

JESSE. (*Offstage.*) There's only bananas on top of the refrigerator.

MARÍA PILAR. *Ay San Fernando de los Flojos*, when will you cure that lazy child? *Con permiso*, Doña Luisa. (*She starts to leave. Grabbing María Pilar by the sleeve, Luisa Ruiz points to the window of her own house.*)

LUISA RUIZ. There she is. There's Esmerelda. You see her? Eh, you see her?

MARÍA PILAR. Yes, yes Doña Luisa, I can see her.

LUISA RUIZ. I call her "La Princesa," she's a real snob, that one, just like royalty. Sits there all day.

MARÍA PILAR. That's because the dog is blind, Doña Luisa. And you should . . .

LUISA RUIZ. (*Interrupting.*) They gave her to me that time I was an extra in the movies . . . the man said that she was the daughter of Lassie and she had belonged to La Liz Taylor.

MARÍA PILAR. You should take that animal to the veterinarian and . . .

LUISA RUIZ. (*Interrupting.*) It's the cataracts in her eyes. I can cure that. I know there is something I can use to cure that.

MARÍA PILAR.. (*walking briskly to house.*) Jesse! Jesse! María de Jesús. (*Jesse comes out the back door. She looks disheveled.*)

JESSE. Mom! Don't call me that.

MARÍA PILAR. Ay, if your Sainted Father *que Dios lo tenga en la Gloria* . . . (*Crosses herself.*) could see you now. Jesse, *por favor*, stand up straight and comb your hair. (*She exits into house.*)

JESSE. What for? I'm not going anyplace. I never go anyplace. Nobody even knows that I'm alive. (*Jesse slumps her way to Luisa Ruiz, who is busy studying the sky.*) I'm just drifting.

LUISA RUIZ. (*Looking at sky.*) Like a cloud.

JESSE. (*Looking at sky.*) Yeah.

LUISA RUIZ. (*No longer looking up.*) It was such a little cloud.

JESSE. (*Still looking at sky.*) A baby cloud, all fat and happy. . . .

LUISA RUIZ. But it got bigger and bigger . . .

JESSE. (*Looking up.*) It didn't know what to do, what to say. It wasn't ready. . . .

LUISA RUIZ. . . . and bigger until it blinded her.

JESSE. (*Looking at Luisa Ruiz.*) Huh?

LUISA RUIZ. The clouds in Esmerelda's eyes.

JESSE. The cataracts.

LUISA RUIZ. I put the pollen of the yellow passion flower on them, which is very strong, Jesse, they say within the flower are the symbols of the crucified Christ.

JESSE. I knew you were talking about the cataracts.

LUISA RUIZ. But it had no effect. I made a tea of that weed they call Juan Simón. . . . (*Raphael appears, lurking around the edge of the yard.*) It had no effect, but I still have the ginseng root in the shape of a cross. . . . (*She starts walking back to her house, mumbling to herself.*) The ginseng root with the leaf of the aloe plant. . . . (*She exits.*)

JESSE. (*Yelling to Raphael.*) My sister's not home! She's not interested in you. She's going to see the world. So you can stop hanging around the house. (*Jesse and Raphael stand, stare at each other for a beat. Jesse picks up a rock. Exit Raphael.*)

Jesse shouts after him.) And you can stop calling on the phone and hanging up. I know it's you . . . (*Softly.*) I recognize your breathing.

First Night

Lights change to night. The stage is dark, except for a large three-quarter moon and the small light in the bedroom window of the Luna house. We hear crickets and the howling of a dog. Enter Rosalinda from the house, in sweatshirt and pants.

ROSALINDA. (*Running in place.*) I'm going to run around the world, over oceans and islands and continents. I'm going to jump over the Himalayas, skip the Spanish Steps and dip my toes in the Blue Nile. I'm going to see places I've never seen and meet people I've never known, Laplanders, Indonesians, Ethiopians. . . . (*Pointing and waving to imaginary people.*) Ay, mira los Japoneses, y los Chinitos and who are those giants? *Ay Dios, los Samoans!* And I will speak many tongues like the Bible. . . . (*Shaking hands with imaginary people.*) *Mucho gusto, yo soy* Rosalinda. *Je suis* Rosalinda, *comment allez-vous? Io sono* Rosalinda. *Jumbo!* Me Rosalinda from America. (*Jesse appears in window. The alarm clock in Jesse's hand goes off.*) Shhhh! Somebody might hear me.
JESSE. Somebody might mug you.
ROSALINDA. I'm too fast. (*She gets into starting position.*)
JESSE. Jeez, I wish we had a stopwatch. It's hard with this alarm clock. . . . Which way are you going tonight?
ROSALINDA. The northern route. Over the Pole.
JESSE. Say hello to the Eskimos.
ROSALINDA. Oh please, Jesse, hurry up.
JESSE. OK, OK. When the little hand hits twelve . . . on your mark . . . get set . . . go!
ROŞALINDA. (*Running.*) There's Fresno . . . San Francisco . . . Portland. . . . (*She exits.*)
JESSE. Weird. (*Enter Raphael. Seeing him, Jesse hides behind window curtain. Raphael paces up and down in front of the house,*

13

looking at the window. He picks up a small stone and throws it through window. Loudly, from behind curtain.) Hey!

RAPHAEL. Psst . . . Rosalinda . . . Rosalinda . . .

JESSE.. (*In a breathy, sexy voice.*) Yeeesss?

RAPHAEL. Rosalinda, I know you got things on your mind with your big race on Saturday *pero* a man can only be ignored so much. (*Pause*) Listen, Rosalinda, *me voy a declarar. Sí*, I'm going to declare myself. (*Pause.*) "Rosalinda": a poem by Raphael Antonia Piña.

You are once

You are twice

You are three times a lady

And that is why you'll always

Be my one and only baby.

When I see you running

Running through the barrio

With your legs so brown and fine

Oh Rosalinda, Rosalinda,

Won't you be mine?

JESSE. (*Throwing a shoe out the window.*) Oh Christ.

RAPHAEL. Ay, Rosy, don't be mean.

JESSE. Her name isn't Rosy. So stop calling her Rosy. She's not gonna answer to Rosy.

RAPHAEL. Oh, you again.

JESSE. Ay Rosalinda! Quick somebody hold me back, I'm about to declare myself.

RAPHAEL. Listen you . . . you . . .

JESSE. My name is Jesse. I live here too ya know.

RAPHAEL. Where is Rosalinda?

JESSE. She's not home. She's running. She's in training and she doesn't see boys when she's training.

RAPHAEL. I'm not a boy, I'm a man.

JESSE. Oh yeah! . . . Well . . . eh . . . er . . . you're not her type. (*Raphael starts to exit.*) Hey Raphael!

RAPHAEL. Yeah.

JESSE. You know your poem?

RAPHAEL. Yeah.

JESSE. It wasn't bad.

RAPHAEL. Thanks. . . . Good night Jesse. (*He exits.*)

JESSE. Good night Raphael Antonio Piña.

ROSALINDA. (*Offstage.*) Mexico City, Acapulco, Puerto Vallarta, La Paz, Santa Rosalia, Encinada . . . (*She enters.*) Tijuana, San Diego, La Orange County, Los Angeles . . . Castro Street. (*Looking up at Jesse.*) How did I do?
JESSE. Huh . . . ? I . . . I lost track. (*Rosalinda sighs and gets into starting position again.*)
ROSALINDA. OK, one more time.
JESSE. Go!
ROSALINDA. (*Running.*) Santa Barbara, San Jose, San Francisco . . . (*She exits running. Rosalinda's voice is heard sounding further and further away, as lights slowly change to day. Continued; offstage.*) Seattle, Portland, Vancouver, Alaska, the Bering Strait, Russia . . .

Second Day

Early morning. Same large sun as First Day. María Pilar, wearing a fresh housedress and apron, is standing in front of her house, scanning the street. Luisa Ruiz, wearing the same outfit as on 1st Day, is coming out of her house.

MARÍA PILAR. Rosalinda! Rosalinda!
LUISA RUIZ. *Buenos días*, María Pilar.
MARÍA PILAR. *Buenos días*, Doña Luisa.
LUISA RUIZ. It's a beautiful day *con mucho viento*. Some people call it the Santa Ana wind. Some people call it the Devil Wind. Some people call it *El Siroco*. And some people —
MARÍA PILAR. *Sí sí*, it's a very windy day. Rosalinda! Running, running, that's all that girl thinks about. Ay and my stomach secreting the acid all morning.
LUISA RUIZ. Running, running that's all El Bobo and Pepe think about too. They wake up, sniff the air and off they go. I think it's something they smell in Mrs. Amador's rose garden. Maybe it's a dead bird. (*She sniffs the air.*) No. Maybe Mrs. Amador is making *chicharrones* . . . (*She sniffs the air*) No . . . (*She sniffs more thoughtfully.*) It must be that patch of

wild peppermint. They say the scent is very invigorating. Maybe that's where La Rosalinda is.

MARÍA PILAR. Doña Luisa, my daughter does not have the custom to go smelling things in other people's garden.

LUISA RUIZ. Oh.

MARÍA PILAR. She runs to practice.

LUISA RUIZ. Oh.

MARÍA PILAR. She runs because this Saturday she is entered in Our Lady of a Thousand Sorrows Marathon.

LUISA RUIZ. No! . . . *Sí?*

MARÍA PILAR. *Sí,* Father Estefan himself went from door to door to collect money for her entrance fee.

LUISA RUIZ. Oh, *pero* he didn't ask me for money. He never came to my door.

MARÍA PILAR. *Válgame Dios,* three hundred young girls from all the Catholic Diocese in California. Ay, I don't know what those priests can be thinking. All that running shakes up a woman's insides.

LUISA RUIZ. He never came to my door. . . . I didn't give anything. . . . This Saturday? . . . That's tomorrow.

MARÍA PILAR. They are making them run from Elysian Park to the Mission downtown.

LUISA RUIZ. Oh. That's far . . . El Bobo could run that far.

MARÍA PILAR. It's not for dogs. It's for Catholic girls.

LUISA RUIZ. Maybe it's not too late for me to give . . .

MARÍA PILAR. I cannot give to her the things she wants. I am a woman alone. Now if her Sainted Father, *que Dios lo tenga en la Gloria* . . . (*Crosses herself.*) were down her with us today . . .

LUISA RUIZ. But it is important to give.

MARÍA PILAR. To give, ah *sí,* to give, *mira no más,* it's easy for you to say give . . . and for him, my husband . . . (*Raising her hand to heaven.*) *charlando* up there, playing the big macho with all the angels and the saints . . . does he listen when Rosalinda says she wants to be educated . . . she wants to see the world? Does he lift a finger? Does he put in a good word for us? No, *se hace sordo,* he pretends not to hear me. *Gracias a Dios,* Rosalinda knows how to work. She gets that from me.

LUISA RUIZ. She looks so pretty working at La Dairy Queen in her white uniform, just like a nurse. She always gives me free cones, soft-serve she calls it. She goes up to that big steel machine, she presses the red button, and zas! Out comes the ice cream, like a clean white snake it comes round and round and round. Rosalinda twirls the cone. She never spills a drop. When it just gets so high she stops, just like that. She never spills a drop. Then she leans over the counter, with a big smile, and says, "This is for you, Doña Luisa." That girl knows how to give.

MARÍA PILAR. I cry, I beg him, "Juanito, *mi amor*," I say, "help us. It's our duty as parents to provide for our children. *Por favor, Papacito lindo*, I'm already sewing ten hours a day just to put food in our mouths." Did I hear from him? Nothing. *Ni una palabra. Condenado viejo*. . . . It took Father Estefan to put her in this race. Just think if she wins *el gran premio* it is a trip to Rome and all the expenses paid . . . but he . . . (*Indicating husband in heaven*.) didn't even help me with the entrance fee or the Nike running shoes. Father Estefan himself had to go door-to-door.

LUISA RUIZ. (*To María Pilar's husband in heaven*.) I swear he never came to my door.

MARÍA PILAR. She has to run like a dog to get somewhere in life. Ay, this acid is killing me. Jesse!

LUISA RUIZ. Run like a dog . . .?

MARÍA PILAR. Jesse, the Rolaids. (*Jesse is coming out the back door, looking more disheveled than usual*.)

JESSE. I can't find them Mom.

MARÍA PILAR. María de Jesús! Look at you! *Por favor*, do something. Comb your hair. Stand up straight. Be a señorita. (*Exit María Pilar into house. Jesse walks up to the fence and Luisa Ruiz*).

JESSE. Please stop calling me that! It's weird. . . . I was real cute until I was twelve . . . people always pinching my cheeks. (*Pinching her own cheeks*.) "Ay qué preciosa!" "Ay qué belleza." But now it's all this pressure.

LUISA RUIZ. Run like a dog. . . .

JESSE. Yeah, far away. . . . No, wouldn't do any good, I think it's some kinda contagious disease, no matter where you go people expect you to comb your hair and stand up straight. I try, but my hair keeps falling into my face and my body just has this . . . terminal slouch . . . it's like I got a hunchback's blood . . . or—

MARÍA PILAR. (*Offstage.*) Jesse! Jesse! What is this *porquería* under your bed?

JESSE. Maybe I wasn't meant to be a señorita.

MARÍA PILAR. (*Offstage*) Dr. Pepper, Twinkies, Cheetos . . . (*Jesse sighs and slumps her way into the house.*)

LUISA RUIZ. She has to run like a dog. . . . (*She exits slowly toward her house.*)

MARÍA PILAR. (*Offstage.*) Snickers, Ding-Dongs, Ho-Ho's, Susie-Qs, a pizza! (*Maria Pilar's voice fades. Light changes to night.*)

Second Night

Moon is fuller than First Night, but not yet full. There is a soft, low-energy sound under this scene, like something vibrating.

Luisa Ruiz, wearing a dark kimono, is standing in front of her doorway. She is holding her hands in front of her body, with a red flannel cloth over them. Raphael appears, lurking around the edges of the yard. Seeing Luisa Ruiz, he hides behind the jacaranda tree. As Rosalinda comes out of her house in her running outfit, Luisa Ruiz beckons to her with both hands and the red flannel cloth. This gesture is slow, as though she is hypnotizing Rosalinda.)

LUISA RUIZ. *Ancho y profundo en pasos en el corazón en al Espíritu Santo. Espíritu Bendito.* (*Rosalinda slowly waves to Luisa Ruiz and stands before her. Luisa Ruiz makes the sign of the cross on Rosalinda. Rosalinda kneels in front of Luisa Ruiz, who then opens her hands and carefully holds out a special Yu-Yu amulet—a small red flannel bag, the size of a large book of matches, which is filled with special herbs and potions and hung around the neck by a drawstring. Luisa Ruiz holds the Yu-Yu high above her own head.) Niño Santo Lobo.* (*She brings the Yu-Yu*

18

down and hangs it around Rosalinda's neck as she starts her chant
over and around Rosalinda.)
Cristo Santo de los Lagos y las Montañas dice—
   (She claps.)
Madre Santa de las Valles dice—
   (Clap.)
Padre Santo de la Sombra y el Sol dice—
   (Clap.)
Virgencita de la Niebla dice—
   (Clap.)
Niño Santo de las Criaturas dice—
   (Clap.)
Santa Ana de los Vientos Secos dice—
   (Clap.)
Espíritu Santo de la Chupa Rosa dice—
   (Clap.)
Espíritu Santo de la Mariposa dice—
   (Clap.)
San Bernardo de los Perros dice—
   (Clap.)
Dios te bendiga
Cristo Santo te bendiga.
(We hear a dog howl. Raphael exits. Low-energy sound fades into
sound of TV cartoons as lights change to day.)

Third Day

Early morning. Some large sun as First and Second Days.
Sound of TV cartoons continues. María Pilar comes out
from her house.

MARÍA PILAR. Rosalinda! *(Yells toward house.)* Jesse! Jesse!
Turn off those cartoons, you hear me? I want you to go after
your sister.
JESSE. *(In the window.)* Mom . . . it's seven o'clock. It's
Saturday.
MARÍA PILAR. Now, Jesse. Do you hear me?
JESSE. Jeez, what's the big deal? *(Jesse disappears from win-*
dow. Sound of cartoons goes off.)

19

MARÍA PILAR. Your sister has to come back here and have a good breakfast. Then we have to go to la special mass for the runners where Father Estefan is going to bless her feet before the race. *Andale*, Jesse. Hurry up. (*Jesse comes out, looking very sleepy, wearing her pajamas with a skirt on top.*)
JESSE. I don't believe this.
MARÍA PILAR. You don't believe anything *y mira no más*, how you look. At your age I was up at five. I was already washed, dressed and making tortillas for all the men in the house.
JESSE. (*Rolling up pj legs.*) Take it easy, Mom, I'm going. (*She exits.*)
MARÍA PILAR. (*Calling after Jesse.*) And stop at the market and get some orange juice for your sister. Tell them to charge it to my account . . . and tell them I'll pay them next week. (*To husband in heaven.*) Ay, Juanito, you better keep your eye on that child.
ORLANDO. (*Enters.*) *Reader's Digest* . . . bill from Dr. Mirabel. . . . *Buenos días*, María Pilar. (*Handing her mail.*) Well today's the big day . . . eh. And the whole barrio's gonna be there. How's Rosalinda?
MARÍA PILAR. Ay Orlando, how do I know? I am only her mother, I am the last person to know where she is or how she is. Have you seen Rosalinda?
ORLANDO. Now don't start worrying, she's just warming up for the big race . . . whew! *Qué* hot . . . looks like it's going to be another scorcher.
MARÍA PILAR. Running, running. The whole thing is affecting my nerves.
ORLANDO. It's the Santa Ana winds, they affect people.
MARÍA PILAR. *Por favor* Orlando, if you see her tell her to come home.
ORLANDO. Of course María Pilar, "Go home at once," that's what I'll tell her. (*Turning to go.*) See you at the race. (*He exits.*)
MARÍA PILAR. (*Walking to house.*) Big race or no big race a person should tell their mother, a person should eat their breakfast. (*Exit María Pilar. Sun moves up a fraction in sky to indicate passage of time. Rosalinda zooms past the house. Enter*

Jesse, running, carrying a paper bag; one of her pj legs has fallen down.)

JESSE. Amaa! Amaa!

MARÍA PILAR. (*Comes out of house.*) *Ay por Dios*, Jesse, walk *como una dama . . . un* lady.

JESSE. Ma, wait'll I tell you what Rosalinda did.

MARÍA PILAR. And where's your sister? Did you tell her about la special mass?

JESSE. I tried, Mom, but she just barked at me. OK. I'm walking down Castro Street. I'm right in front of Arganda's Garage. When Manny Arganda slides out from under a '68 Chevy, stands up and says, "Hey Essé, what's with jur seester?" I tell him to drop dead. He says, "OK. Essé, hab a nice dey." He thinks he's so cool.

MARÍA PILAR. Jesse.

JESSE. OK, OK. That's when I see Rosalinda, with Pepe and Bobo. I yell at her, I say, "Rosalinda, Mom says to come home," that's when she barked at me. Then she turns around and runs up to this car. . . . It was a black Impala with a little red racing stripe all along the side and real pretty red letters on the door that said "Danny Little Red Lopez."

MARÍA PILAR. *Por favor* Jesse.

JESSE. OK, OK. So she runs up to the car, and Mom . . . you won't believe this . . . she jumps over the car! . . . The black Impala, she jumps over it! . . . Just like la Wonder Woman . . . and she wasn't even breathing hard.

MARÍA PILAR. Jesse, why do you lie?

JESSE. Mom, it's exactly what happened. And when I went to the market they said Rosalinda charged a pound of chopped meat and bones.

MARÍA PILAR. That's ridiculous. Your sister never eats meat. Didn't you tell her to get home and about the mass?

JESSE. I couldn't catch her. She's so fast. The last time I saw her she's standing by the stoplight going like this. . . . (*Does an imitation of a dog running in place. Paws out, tongue out like a dog, panting.*)

MARÍA PILAR. Ave María Santísima, I told her never to bounce like that. She's gonna break her eggs.

JESSE. Not eggs, chopped beef.

MARÍA PILAR. I'm talking about her ovaries.

JESSE. Ovaries?

MARÍA PILAR. She's going to ruin her ovaries running like that.

JESSE. Ah Mom, I'm sure . . .

MARÍA PILAR. *La verdad!* Any doctor will tell you bouncing and riding a motorcycle is going to break your eggs.

JESSE. Uuggh. Disgusting. I'm going in for a soda.

MARÍA PILAR. No señorita, not before your breakfast.

JESSE. Eeewww Mom, please, I don't want breakfast. I just want a soda.

MARÍA PILAR. All right baby, all right. You stay here in case your sister runs by and I'll get you the soda . . . but don't drink it too fast. If you drink ice-cold soda too fast it gives you bad gas.

JESSE. Mom!

MARÍA PILAR. Ah *sí*, you laugh *pero* I've known people who have died of these things. (*Exits to house.*)

JESSE. Oh yeah? When I'm eighteen I'm going to ride a big black Harley Davidson motorcycle that has "La Jesse" painted on the side of the gas tank. I'll be jumping over cars, zooming along dusty, bumpy desert trails, and doing loop-dee-loos on the Ventura Freeway. All this, while drinking an ice . . . cold . . . soda real fast before breakfast! (*We hear the sound of a pack of dogs barking and see Rosalinda running from* U.L. *to* U.R. — *a flash of her flying, wild black hair as she runs by. Jesse runs after Rosalinda.*) Rosalinda! Rosalinda! (*As she exits.*) Rosalinda Mom says for you — (*More barking. Offstage.*) Rosalinda wait . . . ! (*María Pilar runs out the back door with a bottle of soda and a glass in her hands.*)

MARÍA PILAR. Jesse . . .! Rosalinda . . .! Come back here. This is no time to be playing. (*María Pilar runs around the back of the house and comes out in front. Enter Mrs. Amador. She is out of breath, her hair is askew. She is splattered with mud and rose petals. She carries a broken rosebush. She leans against the fence, trying to catch her breath.*) Señora! *Qué le pasa?* (*Out of breath, Mrs. Amador struggles to speak.*) *Andale* Mrs. Amador, make an effort. Speak to me.

22

MRS. AMADOR. Rosalinda . . .! The dogs . . .!

MARÍA PILAR. *Qué? Qué? Qué dices de* Rosalinda?

MRS. AMADOR. Rosalinda *y los perros* destroyed my rose garden.

MARÍA PILAR. No . . . No . . .

MRS. AMADOR. *Sí, sí,* all my roses. La Yellow Rose de Texas . . . las tea roses, La Eleanor Roosevelt . . . La Jacqueline Kennedy . . . *y esta* . . . (*Holding up broken rosebush.*) La Mamie Eisenhower. (*The sound of dogs barking is heard.*) Here they come . . . here they come . . . (*Rosalinda runs through,* U.R. *to* U.L., *followed by a worn-out Jesse.*)

JESSE. (*Running to her mother.*) Mom, Mom you should see Rosalinda! She's chasing cars down Castro Street! She's . . . !

MRS. AMADOR. (*Interrupting.*) You should see what she did to my rose garden!!

MARÍA PILAR. I'm telling you it was those dogs next door.

MRS. AMADOR. *Pero* Rosalinda was with them! She was one of them. All wild-looking she was *así, mira* . . . (*Baring her teeth, imitating Rosalinda's wild look.*) Ay! And blood all around her mouth. (*Crossing herself.*) It makes me tremble to think of it.

MARÍA PILAR. Blood around her mouth.

JESSE. Aw Mom, that was just from the raw meat she was eating. (*Enter Orlando, in a state of disarray, strap on mailbag broken, pants leg torn.*)

ORLANDO. La Rosalinda *se freakió.*

MARÍA PILAR. Where is she!? Where did she go?

JESSE. She's OK, Mom, she's over at the park catching frisbees between her teeth. She's really good. You should see her.

MRS. AMADOR. She's on drugs. I've seen it. They go crazy.

JESSE. She's not crazy.

MARÍA PILAR. (*Crying.*) She can't even take Contac.

MRS. AMADOR. That's how they start. First the Contac and then the — (*Luisa Ruiz enters to her front yard.*)

LUISA RUIZ. Pepe! Pepe! Bobo! (*Enter Raphael running.*)

RAPHAEL. Jesse! Jesse! Rosalinda's in . . . (*Seeing Luisa*

Ruiz and pointing at her.) She's the one! La Dog Lady! She gave her something. She put a curse on her. She turned her into a dog! I seen her do it.

MARÍA PILAR. (*To Luisa Ruiz.*) What have you done to my daughter?

MRS. AMADOR. Drugs! She gave her drugs. She's a pusher.

RAPHAEL. I seen her. She put something around her neck. And said spooky words over her.

MARÍA PILAR. (*Taking Luisa Ruiz by the shoulders, shaking her.*) What did you do to Rosalinda? What did you give her?

MRS. AMADOR. Speed! I bet that's what she gave her.

ORLANDO. (*Pulling María Pilar away from Luisa Ruiz.*) Give her a chance to talk. *Orale*, Doña Luisa. Did you give Rosalinda something?

LUISA RUIZ. She had to run like a dog . . . I gave her the Spirit . . . the Dog Spirit. It won't hurt her.

MRS. AMADOR. (*Crossing herself.*) Devil's work. *Ave, Dios,* she's a *bruja,* a witch. Where's my cross? (*Searching for cross at her neck.*) Jesse! Don't look at her. (*Pulling Jesse's face away.*) Nobody look at her eyes. (*All shield their eyes, except Orlando.*)

ORLANDO. *Cálmanse! Y* stop talking nonsense.

MRS. AMADOR. *Qué* nonsense and *qué nada!* Didn't Father Estefan himself say that she made the dog in the window blind with all them herbs she put in the dog's eyes? Didn't he? Didn't he?

MARÍA PILAR. *Sí, sí,* he said to keep away from her. (*Crying.*) She's turned my daughter into a dog.

JESSE. Mom! (*Raphael, shielding his eyes, pulls a switchblade and points it at Luisa Ruiz's throat.*)

RAPHAEL. Turn her back, Dog Lady.

ORLANDO. Raphael . . . put it away. Now everybody calm down. It's just these damn Santa winds. It drives people crazy.

JESSE. She's not crazy.

MARÍA PILAR. *Por favor* Doña Luisa, you're a powerful woman. . . . I beg you, bring me back my daughter. (*Luisa Ruiz rummages in her pockets and pulls out an ultrasonic dog whistle. As she pulls it out, everybody stands back. She blows it. Mrs. Amador crosses herself, gasps, and points across the street.*)

MRS. AMADOR. Ay! *Mira* Mr. Mura's garage door opened

all by itself. (*They all turn around and look in shocked silence. Raphael drops his knife. One by one all cross themselves, except for Luisa Ruiz and Jesse. Jesse stands up on the fence and looks up and down the street.*)

JESSE. Here she comes. Wow! Rosalinda that was great. (*Rosalinda enters running. She continues running in place. Her hair is messy and wild. She is splattered with mud and rose petals. She has a keenly determined look in her eyes and holds a frisbee between her teeth.*)

MARÍA PILAR. Rosalinda, where were you? And why didn't you come when I called? (*Rosalinda drops frisbee at María Pilar's feet.*) No señorita, I'm not playing games with you.

MRS. AMADOR. (*Passing her hands before Rosalinda's face.*) Rosalinda . . . how do you feel?

JESSE. Fine! She feels fine!

ORLANDO. You're all right, eh Rosalinda?

JESSE. Of course she's all right.

MARÍA PILAR. Rosalinda, I want you to go to bed.

JESSE. Not now, she'll be late for the race, Ready? Rome, here comes Rosalinda. (*Exit Rosalinda, running. The others look at one another. Then all run offstage after Rosalinda, except for Luisa Ruiz, and Raphael, who lags slowly behind.*)

RAPHAEL. (*Exiting slowly.*) A man can only take so much. She's never home, she's a lot of trouble, running, jumping, barking. Women! (*Luisa Ruiz stands onstage alone for a beat. We hear the sound of dogs barking. She goes to the alleyway.*)

LUISA RUIZ. Pepe! Bobo! No, you can't go . . . it's only for Catholic girls. We're not invited. (*She runs offstage after the dogs.*)

Third Night

There is a full moon. The sound of a mariachi band playing "Guadalahara," and other party sounds. María Pilar in front of her house, in a party dress, hanging a banner proclaiming "Rosalinda Number One." Enter Mrs. Amador carrying a big plate.

MRS. AMADOR. *Tamales estilo Jalisco.*

MARÍA PILAR. Just think, she's going to Rome and all the expenses paid.

MRS. AMADOR. What about the woof! woof! (*Rosalinda comes out of the house. Mrs. Amador jumps back and looks at Rosalinda very cautiously.*)

ROSALINDA. She hasn't come yet? She said she would come.

MARÍA PILAR. Now don't get excited, if Doña Luisa said she would come, then she will come.

MRS. AMADOR. *Sí*, don't get excited. Nothing to get excited about.

ROSALINDA. Oh Mom, isn't it wonderful! I'm going to see the world. (*Looking up at the sky.*) I'm going to see the universe. . . . I am going to dance on Venus, skate on Saturn's rings, dive into the Milky Way and wash my hair with stars.

MRS. AMADOR. Is she getting excited? (*Rosalinda and María Pilar are looking up to the sky. Seeing them, Mrs. Amador very cautiously starts to look up.*)

MARÍA PILAR. Ay Juanito . . . I feel your soft brown eyes on me . . . on Rosalinda . . . on Jesse . . . Jesse? Rosalinda, where's Jesse?

ROSALINDA. (*Still gazing at the sky.*) I don't know Mom.

MRS. AMADOR. (*Eyeing the sky with great suspicion.*) Is somebody there? (*Mrs. Amador continues to stare straight up to the sky throughout the rest of this scene. Enter Orlando and Raphael, both very dressed up. Raphael carries a big bouquet of flowers.*)

ORLANDO. *Orale*, Rafa, give her the flowers.

RAPHAEL. Now?

MARÍA PILAR. Ay look Rosalinda, it's Orlando and Raphael. . . . *Pasen, pasen* . . . ay, where is Jesse?

Rosalinda. I'll get her. (*Rosalinda goes toward house as Luisa Ruiz comes out of her house in a faded cocktail dress, a large flower in her hair.*)

MARÍA PILAR. *Ay qué bonita se ve, me da tanto gusto a ver* La Doña Luisa.

LUISA RUIZ. Oh! Thank you, María Pilar. (*She looks up to the sky.*) It's a beautiful night.

MARÍA PILAR. *Sí*. God works in mysterious ways, Doña Luisa. (*Enter Jesse. She has been transformed into a beautiful young princess. She stands next to Rosalinda. Raphael stands before them, holding the bouquet of flowers, awestruck at Jesse. All stare at Jesse in silence except for Mrs. Amador, who is still staring at the sky.*)

ORLANDO. Look at La Jesse!

MARÍA PILAR. Ay Juanito. (*She crosses herself.*) She combed her hair.

LUISA RUIZ. She looks just like a princess.

ORLANDO. (*Nudging Raphael.*) Now Rafa! Now. (*Raphael, staring at Jesse, tears the bouquet of flowers in half, giving half to Rosalinda and half to Jesse.*) Y la fiesta pues? . . . I am gonna dance with you, Doña Luisa. (*Orlando takes Luisa Ruiz arm-in-arm and exits into the house as María Pilar moves to Mrs. Amador, who is still staring into the sky, holding plate of tamales.*)

MARÍA PILAR. *Andale*, Mrs. Amador, it's time for the tamales.

MRS. AMADOR. (*Still looking at the sky.*) Is somebody watching us? (*María Pilar takes Mrs. Amador into the house, followed by Raphael.*)

ROSALINDA. I'm proud of you Jesse.

JESSE. (*To Rosalinda.*) You're going to see the world . . . all those places . . . all the things that will happen to you. . . .

ROSALINDA. I'll be back.

JESSE. You'll be different.

ROSALINDA. We're sisters forever.

JESSE. Rosalinda? . . . Can I see it? (*Rosalinda brings out the Yu-Yu from under her blouse.*) Can I touch it? . . . Did . . . did you really turn into a dog?

ROSALINDA. (*Taking Yu-Yu off her neck, holding it in her hands.*) You have to work very hard.

JESSE. I know. (*Rosalinda puts Yu-Yu around Jesse's neck. She exits into the house. Jesse turns around and stares at the moon. She slowly walks up Castro Street toward the moon as lights slowly fade and we hear María Pilar's voice.*)

MARÍA PILAR. (*Offstage.*) Jesse! Jesse!

END OF PLAY

PROPERTY LIST

First Day

Onstage
Rotating sprinkler
Strange plants
Rubber tires
Rubbish
Sign: "CURANDERA – HEALER"
2 mailboxes
Jacaranda tree
Rock

Offstage
Mailbag (Orlando)
Alarm clock (Jesse)
Shoe (Jesse)

First Night

On stage
Small stone

Second Night

Onstage
Red flannel cloth
Yu-Yu amulet

Third Day

Offstage
Paper bag (Jesse)
Bottle of soda and glass (María Pilar)
Broken rosebush (Mrs. Amador)
Switchblade (Raphael)
Ultrasonic dog whistle (Luisa Ruiz)
Frisbee (Rosalinda)

Third Night

Onstage
Banner: "Rosalinda Number One"

Offstage
Big plate of tamales (Mrs. Amador)
Big bouquet of flowers (Raphael)

THE CUBAN
SWIMMER

CHARACTERS

MARGARITA SUÁREZ, the swimmer
EDUARDO SUÁREZ, her father, the coach
SIMÓN SUÁREZ, her brother
AÍDA SUÁREZ, her mother
ABUELA, her grandmother
VOICE OF MEL MUNSON
VOICE OF MARY BETH WHITE
VOICE OF RADIO OPERATOR

Live conga drums can be used to punctuate the action of the play.

TIME
Summer.

PLACE
The Pacific Ocean between San Pedro and Catalina Island.

THE CUBAN SWIMMER

Scene 1

Pacific Ocean. Midday. On the horizon, in perspective, a small boat enters U.L., *crosses to* U.R. *and exits. Pause. Lower on the horizon, the same boat, in larger perspective, enters* U.R., *crosses and exits* U.L. *Blackout.*

Scene 2

Pacific Ocean. Midday. The swimmer, Margarita Suárez, is swimming. On the boat following behind her are her father, Eduardo Suárez, holding a megaphone, and Simón, her brother, sitting on top of the cabin with his shirt off, punk sunglasses on, binoculars hanging on his chest.

EDUARDO. (*Leaning forward, shouting in time to Margarita's swimming.*) *Uno, dos, uno, dos. Y uno, dos* . . . keep your shoulders parallel to the water.

SIMÓN. I'm gonna take these glasses off and look straight into the sun.

EDUARDO. (*Through megaphone.*) *Muy bien, muy bien* . . . but punch those arms in, baby.

SIMÓN. (*Looking directly at the sun through binoculars.*) Come on, come on, zap me. Show me something. (*He looks behind at the shoreline and ahead at the sea.*) Stop! Stop, Papi! Stop! (*Aída Suárez and Abuela, the swimmer's mother and grandmother, enter running from the back of the boat.*)

AÍDA and ABUELA. *Qué? Qué es?*

AÍDA. *Es un* shark?

EDUARDO. Eh?

33

ABUELA. *Que es un* shark *dicen?* (*Eduardo blows whistle. Margarita looks up at the boat.*)

SIMÓN. No, Papi, no shark, no shark. We've reached the halfway mark.

ABUELA. (*Looking into the water.*) *A dónde está?*

AÍDA. It's not in the water.

ABUELA. Oh no? Oh no?

AÍDA. No! *A poco* do you think they're gonna have signs in the water to say you are halfway to Santa Catalina? No. It's done very scientific. *A ver, hijo,* explain it to your grandma.

SIMÓN. Well, you see Abuela — (*He points behind.*) There's San Pedro. (*He points ahead.*) And there's Santa Catalina. Looks halfway to me. (*Abuela shakes her head and is looking back and forth, trying to make the decision, when suddenly the sound of a helicopter is heard.*)

ABUELA. (*Looking up.*) *Virgencita de la Caridad del Cobre. Qué es eso?* (*Sound of helicopter gets closer. Margarita looks up.*)

MARGARITA. Papi, Papi! (*A small commotion on the boat, with everybody pointing at the helicopter above. Shadows of the helicopter fall on the boat. Simón looks up at it through binoculars.*) Papi — *qué es?* What is it?

EDUARDO. (*Through megaphone.*) Uh . . . uh . . . uh *un momentico . . . mi hija.* . . . Your papi's got everything under control, understand? Uh . . . you just keep stroking. And stay . . . uh . . . close to the boat.

SIMÓN. Wow, Papi! We're on TV man! Holy Christ, we're all over the fucking U.S.A.! It's Mel Munson and Mary Beth White!

AÍDA. *Por Dios!* Simón, don't swear. And put on your shirt. (*Aída fluffs her hair, puts on her sunglasses and waves to the helicopter. Simón leans over the side of the boat and yells to Margarita.*)

SIMÓN. Yo, Margo! You're on TV, man.

EDUARDO. Leave your sister alone. Turn on the radio.

MARGARITA. Papi! *Qué está pasando?*

ABUELA. *Que es la televisión dicen?* (*She shakes her head.*) *Porque como yo no puedo ver nada sin mis espejuelos.* (*Abuela rummages through the boat, looking for her glasses. Voices of Mel Munson and Mary Beth White are heard over the boat's radio.*)

MEL'S VOICE. As we take a closer look at the gallant crew

of La Havana . . . and there . . . yes, there she is . . . the little Cuban swimmer from Long Beach, California, nineteen-year-old Margarita Suárez. The unknown swimmer is our Cinderella entry . . . a bundle of tenacity, battling her way through the choppy, murky waters of the cold Pacific to reach the Island of Romance . . . Santa Catalina . . . where should she be the first to arrive, two thousand dollars and a gold cup will be waiting for her.

AÍDA. Doesn't even cover our expenses.

ABUELA. *Qué dice?*

EDUARDO. Shhhh!

MARY BETH'S VOICE. This is really a family effort, Mel, and—

MEL'S VOICE. Indeed it is. Her trainer, her coach, her mentor is her father, Eduardo Suárez. Not a swimmer himself, it says here, Mr. Suárez is head usher of the Holy Name Society and the owner-operator of Suárez Treasures of the Sea and Salvage Yard. I guess it's one of those places . . .

MARY BETH'S VOICE. If I might interject a fact here, Mel, assisting in this swim is Mrs. Suárez who is a former Miss Cuba.

MEL'S VOICE. And a beautiful woman in her own right. Let's try and get a closer look. (*Helicopter sound gets louder. Margarita, frightened, looks up again.*)

MARGARITA. Papi!

EDUARDO. (*Through megaphone.*) *Mi hija*, don't get nervous . . . it's the press. I'm handling it.

AÍDA. I see how you're handling it.

EDUARDO. (*Through megaphone.*) Do you hear? Everything is under control. Get back into your rhythm. Keep your elbows high and kick and kick and kick and kick . . .

ABUELA. (*Finds her glasses and puts them on.*) *Ay sí, es la televisión* . . . (*She points to helicopter.*) *Qué lindo mira* . . . (*She fluffs her hair, gives a big wave.*) *Alo América! Viva mi Margarita, viva todo los Cubanos en los Estados Unidos!*

AÍDA. *Ay por Dios*, Cecilia, the man didn't come all this way in his helicopter to look at you jumping up and down, making a fool of yourself.

ABUELA. I don't care. I'm proud.

AÍDA. He can't understand you anyway.

35

ABUELA. *Viva . . .   (She stops.) Simón, comó se dice viva?*
SIMÓN. Hurray.
ABUELA. Hurray for *mi* Margarita *y* for all the Cubans living *en* the United States, *y un abrazo . . .* Simón, *abrazo . . .*
SIMÓN. A big hug.
ABUELA. *Sí,* a big hug to all my friends in Miami, Long Beach, Union City, except for my son Carlos who lives in New York in sin! He lives . . . *(She crosses herself.)* in Brooklyn with a Puerto Rican woman in sin! *No decente . . .*
SIMÓN. Decent.
ABUELA. Carlos, *no decente.* This family, *decente.*
AÍDA. Cecilia, *por Dios.*
MEL'S VOICE. Look at that enthusiasm. The whole family has turned out to cheer little Margarita on to victory! I hope they won't be too disappointed.
MARY BETH'S VOICE. She seems to be making good time, Mel.
MEL'S VOICE. Yes, it takes all kinds to make a race. And it's a testimonial to the all-encompassing fairness . . . the greatness of this, the Wrigley Invitational Women's Swim to Catalina, where among all the professionals there is still room for the amateurs . . . like these, the simple people we see below us on the ragtag La Havana, taking their long-shot chance to victory. *Vaya con Dios! (Helicopter sound fading as family, including Margarita, watch silently. Static as Simón turns radio off. Eduardo walks to bow of boat, looks out on the horizon.)*
EDUARDO. *(To himself.)* Amateurs.
AÍDA. Eduardo, that person insulted us. Did you hear, Eduardo? That he called us a simple people in a ragtag boat? Did you hear . . . ?
ABUELA. *(Clenching her fist at departing helicopter.) Mal-Rayo los parta!*
SIMÓN. *(Same gesture.)* Asshole! *(Aída follows Eduardo as he goes to side of boat and stares at Margarita.)*
AÍDA. This person comes in his helicopter to insult your wife, your family, your daughter . . .
MARGARITA. *(Pops her head out of the water.)* Papi?
AÍDA. Do you hear me, Eduardo? I am not simple.
ABUELA. *Sí.*

AÍDA. I am complicated.

ABUELA. *Sí, demasiada complicada.*

AÍDA. Me and my family are not so simple.

SIMÓN. Mom, the guy's an asshole.

ABUELA. (*Shaking her fist at helicopter.*) Asshole!

AÍDA. If my daughter was simple she would not be in that water swimming.

MARGARITA. Simple? Papi . . .?

AÍDA. *Ahora*, Eduardo, this is what I want you to do. When we get to Santa Catalina I want you to call the TV station and demand *un* apology.

EDUARDO. *Cállete mujer! Aquí mando yo.* I will decide what is to be done.

MARGARITA. Papi, tell me what's going on.

EDUARDO. Do you understand what I am saying to you, Aída?

SIMÓN. (*Leaning over side of boat, to Margarita.*) Yo Margo! You know that Mel Munson guy on TV? He called you a simple amateur and said you didn't have a chance.

ABUELA. (*Leaning directly behind Simón.*) *Mi hija, insultó a la familia. Desgraciado!!*

AÍDA. (*Leaning in behind Abuela.*) He called us peasants! And your father is not doing anything about it. He just knows how to yell at me.

EDUARDO. (*Through megaphone.*) Shut up! All of you! Do you want to break her concentration? Is that what you are after? Eh? (*Abuela, Aída and Simón shrink back. Eduardo paces before them.*) Swimming is rhythm and concentration. You win a race *aquí.* (*Pointing to his head.*) Now . . . (*To Simón.*) you, take care of the boat, Aída y Mama . . . do something. Anything. Something practical. (*Abuela and Aída get on knees and pray in Spanish.*) *Hija*, give it everything, eh? . . . *por la familia. Uno . . . dos. . . .* You must win. (*Simón goes into cabin. The prayers continue as lights change to indicate bright sunlight, later in the afternoon.*)

Scene 3

Tableau for a couple of beats. Eduardo on bow with timer

*in one hand as he counts strokes per minute. Simón is in
the cabin steering, wearing his sunglasses, baseball cap
on backwards. Abuela and Aída are at the side of the boat,
heads down, hands folded, still muttering prayers in
Spanish.*

AÍDA and ABUELA. (*Crossing themselves.*) *En el nombre del
Padre, del Hijo y del Espíritu Santo amén.*
EDUARDO. (*Through megaphone.*) You're stroking
seventy-two!
SIMÓN. (*Singing.*) Mama's stroking, Mama's stroking
seventy-two . . .
EDUARDO. (*Through megaphone.*) You comfortable with it?
SIMÓN. (*Singing*) Seventy-two, seventy-two, seventy-two
for you.
AÍDA. (*Looking at the heavens.*) *Ay*, Eduardo, *ven acá*, we
should be grateful that *Nuestro* Señor gave us such a beautiful
day.
ABUELA. (*Crosses herself.*) *Sí, gracias a Dios.*
EDUARDO. She's stroking seventy-two, with no problem.
(*He throws a kiss to the sky.*) It's a beautiful day to win.
AÍDA. *Qué hermoso!* So clear and bright. Not a cloud in the
sky. *Mira! Mira!* Even rainbows on the water . . . a sign
from God.
SIMÓN. (*Singing.*) Rainbows on the water . . . you in my
arms . . .
ABUELA and EDUARDO. (*Looking the wrong way.*) *Dónde?*
AÍDA. (*Pointing toward Margarita.*) There, dancing in front
of Margarita, leading her on . . .
EDUARDO. Rainbows on. . . . *Ay coño!* It's an oil slick!
You . . . you . . . (*To Simón.*) Stop the boat. (*Runs to bow,
yelling.*) Margarita! Margarita! (*On the next stroke, Margarita
comes up all covered in black oil.*)
MARGARITA. Papi! Papi! (*Everybody goes to the side and
stares at Margarita, who stares back. Eduardo freezes.*)
AÍDA. *Apúrate* Eduardo, move . . . what's wrong with
you . . . *no me oíste*, get my daughter out of the water.
EDUARDO. (*Softly.*) We can't touch her. If we touch her,
she's disqualified.
AÍDA. But I'm her mother.

38

EDUARDO. Not even by her own mother. Especially by her own mother. . . . You always want the rules to be different for you, you always want to be the exception. (*To Simón*) And you . . . you didn't see it, eh? You were playing again?

SIMÓN. Papi, I was watching . . .

AÍDA. (*Interrupting.*) *Pues,* do something Eduardo. You are the big coach, the monitor.

SIMÓN. Mentor! Mentor!

EDUARDO. How can a person think around you? (*He walks off to bow, puts head in hands.*)

ABUELA. (*Looking over side.*) *Mira como todos los* little birds are dead. (*She crosses herself.*)

AÍDA. Their little wings are glued to their sides.

SIMÓN. Christ, this is like the La Brea tar pits.

AÍDA. They can't move their little wings.

ABUELA. *Esa niña tiene que moverse.*

SIMÓN. Yeah Margo, you gotta move, man. (*Abuela and Simón gesture for Margarita to move. Aída gestures for her to swim.*)

ABUELA. *Anda niña, muévete.*

AÍDA. Swim, *hija,* swim or the *aceite* will stick to your wings.

MARGARITA. Papi?

ABUELA. (*Taking megaphone.*) Your papi say "move it!" (*Margarita with difficulty starts moving.*)

ABUELA, AÍDA and SIMÓN. (*Laboriously counting.*) *Uno, dos . . . uno, dos . . . anda . . . uno, dos.*

EDUARDO. (*Running to take megaphone from Abuela.*) *Uno, dos . . .* (*Simón races into cabin and starts the engine. Abuela, Aída and Eduardo count together.*)

SIMÓN. (*Looking ahead.*)Papi, it's over there!

EDUARDO. Eh?

SIMÓN. (*Pointing ahead and to* R.) It's getting clearer over there.

EDUARDO. (*Through megaphone.*) Now pay attention to me. Go to the right. (*Simón, Abuela, Aída and Eduardo all lean over side. They point ahead and to* R., *except Abuela, who points to* R.)

FAMILY. (*Shouting together.*) *Para yá! Para yá!* (*Lights go down on boat. A special light on Margarita, swimming through the oil, and on Abuela, watching her.*)

ABUELA. *Sangre de mi sangre,* you will be another to save us.

En Bolondron, where your great-grandmother Luz Suárez was born, they say one day it rained blood. All the people, they run into their houses. They cry, they pray, *pero* your great-grandmother Luz she had *cojones* like a man. She run outside. She look straight at the sky. She shake her fist. And she say to the evil one, "*Mira* . . . (*Beating her chest.*) *coño, Diablo, aquí estoy si me quieres.*" And she open her mouth, and she drunk the blood.

(*Blackout.*)

Scene 4

Lights up on boat. Aída and Eduardo are on deck watching Margarita swim.
We hear the gentle, rhythmic lap, lap, lap, of the water, then the sound of inhaling and exhaling as Margarita's breathing becomes louder. Then Margarita's heartbeat is heard, with the lapping of the water and the breathing under it. These sounds continue beneath the dialogue to the end of the scene.

AÍDA. *Dios mío.* Look how she moves through the water . . .
EDUARDO. You see, it's very simple. It is a matter of concentration.
AÍDA. The first time I put her in water she came to life, she grew before my eyes. She moved, she smiled, she loved it more than me. She didn't want my breast any longer. She wanted the water.
EDUARDO. And of course, the rhythm. The rhythm takes away the pain and helps the concentration. (*Pause. Aída and Eduardo watch Margarita.*)
AÍDA. Is that my child, or a seal. . . .
EDUARDO. Ah a seal, the reason for that is that she's keeping her arms very close to her body. She cups her hands and then she reaches and digs, reaches and digs.
AÍDA. To think that a daughter of mine . . .

40

EDUARDO. It's the training, the hours in the water. I used to tie weights around her little wrists and ankles.

AÍDA. A spirit, an ocean spirit, must have entered my body when I was carrying her.

EDUARDO. (*To Margarita.*) Your stroke is slowing down. (*Pause. We hear Margarita's heartbeat with the breathing under, faster now.*)

AÍDA. Eduardo, that night, the night on the boat . . .

EDUARDO. Ah, the night on the boat again . . . the moon was . . .

AÍDA. The moon was full. We were coming to America. . . . *Qué romantico.* (*Heartbeat and breathing continue.*)

EDUARDO. We were cold, afraid, with no money, and on top of everything, you were hysterical, yelling at me, tearing at me with your nails. (*Opens his shirt, points to the base of his neck.*) Look, I still bear the scars . . . telling me that I didn't know what I was doing . . . saying that we were going to die. . . .

AÍDA. You took me, you stole me from my home . . . you didn't give me a chance to prepare. You just said we have to go now, now! Now, you said. You didn't let me take anything. I left everything behind . . . I left everything behind.

EDUARDO. Saying that I wasn't good enough, that your father didn't raise you so that I could drown you in the sea.

AÍDA. You didn't let me say even a goodbye. You took me, you stole me, you tore me from my home.

EDUARDO. I took you so we could be married.

AÍDA. That was in Miami. But that night on the boat, Eduardo. . . . We were not married, that night on the boat.

EDUARDO. *No pasó nada!* Once and for all get it out of your head, it was cold, you hated me and we were afraid. . . .

AÍDA. *Mentiroso!*

EDUARDO. A man can't do it when he is afraid.

AÍDA. Liar! You did it very well.

EDUARDO. I did?

AÍDA. *Sí.* Gentle. You were so gentle and then strong . . . my passion for you so deep. Standing next to you . . . I would ache . . . looking at your hands I would forget to breathe, you were irresistible.

41

EDUARDO. I was?

AÍDA. You took me into your arms, you touched my face with your fingertips . . . you kissed my eyes . . . *la esquina de la boca y* . . .

EDUARDO. *Sí, sí,* and then . . .

AÍDA. I look at your face on top of mine, and I see the lights of Havana in your eyes. That's when you seduced me.

EDUARDO. Shhh, they're gonna hear you. (*Lights go down. Special on Aída.*)

AÍDA. That was the night. A woman doesn't forget those things . . . and later that night was the dream . . . the dream of a big country with fields of fertile land and big, giant things growing. And there by a green, slimy pond I found a giant pea pod and when I opened it, it was full of little, tiny baby frogs. (*Aída crosses herself as she watches Margarita. We hear louder breathing and heartbeat.*)

MARGARITA. Santa Teresa. Little Flower of God, pray for me. San Martín de Porres, pray for me. Santa Rosa de Lima, *Virgencita de la Caridad del Cobre*, pray for me. . . . Mother pray for me.

Scene 5

Loud howling of wind is heard, as lights change to indicate unstable weather, fog and mist. Family on deck, braced and huddled against the wind. Simón is at the helm.

AÍDA. *Ay Dios mío, qué viento.*

EDUARDO. (*Through megaphone.*) Don't drift out . . . that wind is pushing you out. (*To Simón*) You! Slow down. Can't you see your sister is drifting out?

SIMÓN. It's the wind, Papi.

AÍDA. Baby, don't go so far. . . .

ABUELA. (*To heaven.*) *Ay Gran Poder de Dios, quita este maldito viento.*

SIMÓN. Margo! Margo! Stay close to the boat.

EDUARDO. Dig in. Dig in hard. . . . Reach down from your guts and dig in.

ABUELA. (*To heaven.*) Ay Virgen de la Caridad del Cobre, por lo más tú quieres a pararla.

AÍDA. (*Putting her hand out, reaching for Margarita.*) Baby, don't go far. (*Abuela crosses herself. Action freezes. Lights get dimmer, special on Margarita. She keeps swimming, stops, starts again, stops, then, finally exhausted, stops altogether. The boat stops moving.*)

EDUARDO. What's going on here? Why are we stopping?

SIMÓN. Papi, she's not moving! Yo Margo! (*The family all run to the side.*)

EDUARDO. Hija! . . . Hijita! You're tired, eh?

AÍDA. *Por supuesto* she's tired. I like to see you get in the water, waving your arms and legs from San Pedro to Santa Catalina. A person isn't a machine, a person has to rest.

SIMÓN. Yo, Mama! Cool out, it ain't fucking brain surgery.

EDUARDO. (*To Simón*) Shut up, you. (*Louder to Margarita.*) I guess your mother's right for once, huh? . . . I guess you had to stop, eh? . . . Give your brother, the idiot . . . a chance to catch up with you.

SIMÓN. (*Clowning like Mortimer Snurd.*) Dum dee dum dee dum ooops, ah shucks. . . .

EDUARDO. I don't think he's Cuban.

SIMÓN. (*Like Ricky Ricardo.*) Oye Lucy! I'm home! Ba ba lu!

EDUARDO. (*Joins in clowning, grabbing Simón in a headlock.*) What am I gonna do with this idiot, eh? I don't understand this idiot. He's not like us Margarita. (*Laughing.*) You think if we put him into your bathing suit with a cap on his head . . . (*He laughs hysterically.*) you think anyone would know . . . huh? Do you think anyone would know? (*Laughs.*)

SIMÓN. (*Vamping.*) Ay, mi amor. Anybody looking for tits would know. (*Eduardo slaps Simón across the face, knocking him down. Aída runs to Simón's aid. Abuela holds Eduardo back.*)

MARGARITA. *Mía culpa! Mía culpa!*

ABUELA. *Qué dices hija?*

MARGARITA. Papi, it's my fault, it's all my fault. . . . I'm so cold, I can't move. . . . I put my face in the water . . . and I hear them whispering . . . laughing at me. . . .

AÍDA. Who is laughing at you?

43

MARGARITA. The fish are all biting me . . . they hate me . . . they whisper about me. She can't swim, they say. She can't glide. She has no grace. . . . Yellowtails, bonita, tuna, man-o'-war, snub-nose sharks, los baracudas . . . they all hate me . . . only the dolphins care . . . and sometimes I hear the whales crying . . . she is lost, she is dead. I'm so numb, I can't feel. Papi! Papi! Am I dead?

EDUARDO. *Vamos*, baby, punch those arms in. Come on . . . do you hear me?

MARGARITA. Papi . . . Papi . . . forgive me. . . . (*All is silent on the boat. Eduardo drops his megaphone, his head bent down in dejection. Abuela, Aída, Simón all leaning over the side of the boat. Simón slowly walks away.*)

AÍDA. *Mi hija, qué tienes?*

SIMÓN. Oh Christ, don't make her say it. Please don't make her say it.

ABUELA. Say what? *Qué cosa?*

SIMÓN. She wants to quit, can't you see she's had enough?

ABUELA. *Mira, para eso. Esta niña* is turning blue.

AÍDA. *Oyeme, mi hija.* Do you want to come out of the water?

MARGARITA. Papi?

SIMÓN. (*To Eduardo*) She won't come out until *you* tell her.

AÍDA. Eduardo . . . answer your daughter.

EDUARDO. *Le dije* to concentrate . . . concentrate on your rhythm. Then the rhythm would carry her . . . ay it's a beautiful thing, Aída. It's like yoga, like meditation, the mind over matter . . . the mind controlling the body . . . that's how the great things in the world have been done. I wish you . . . I wish my wife could understand.

MARGARITA. Papi?

SIMÓN. (*To Margarita*) Forget him.

AÍDA. (*Imploring.*) Eduardo, *por favor.*

EDUARDO. (*Walking in circles.*) Why didn't you let her concentrate? Don't you understand, the concentration, the rhythm is everything. But no, you wouldn't listen. (*Screaming to the ocean.*) Goddam Cubans, why, God, why do you make us go everywhere with our families? (*He goes to back of boat.*)

AÍDA. (*Opening her arms.*) Mi hija, ven, come to Mami. (*Rocking.*) Your mami knows. (*Abuela has taken the training bottle,*

44

puts it in a net. She and Simón lower it to Margarita.)

SIMÓN. Take this. Drink it. (*As Margarita drinks, Abuela crosses herself.*)

ABUELA. *Sangre de mi sangre.* (*Music comes up softly. Margarita drinks, gives the bottle back, stretches out her arms, as if on a cross. Floats on her back. She begins a graceful backstroke. Lights fade on boat as special lights come up on Margarita. She stops. Slowly turns over and starts to swim, gradually picking up speed. Suddenly as if in pain she stops, tries again, then stops in pain again. She becomes disoriented and falls to the bottom of the sea. Special on Margarita at the bottom of the sea.*)

MARGARITA. *Ya no puedo* . . . I can't . . . A person isn't a machine . . . *es mi culpa* . . . Father forgive me . . . Papi! Papi! One, two. *Uno, dos.* (*Pause.*) Papi! *A dónde estás?* (*Pause.*) One, two, one, two. Papi! Ay Papi! Where are you . . . ? Don't leave me. . . . Why don't you answer me? (*Pause. She starts to swim, slowly.*) *Uno, dos, uno, dos.* Dig in, dig in. (*Stops swimming.*) *Por favor,* Papi! (*Starts to swim again.*) One, two, one, two. Kick from your hip, kick from your hip. (*Stops swimming. Starts to cry.*) Oh God, please. . . . (*Pause.*) Hail Mary, full of grace . . . dig in, dig in . . . the Lord is with thee. . . . (*She swims to the rhythm of her Hail Mary.*) Hail Mary, full of grace . . . dig in, dig in, . . . the Lord is with thee . . . dig in, dig in. . . . Blessed art thou among women. . . . Mommie it hurts. You let go of my hand. I'm lost. . . . And blessed is the fruit of thy womb, now and at the hour of our death. Amen. I don't want to die, I don't want to die. (*Margarita is still swimming. Blackout. She is gone.*)

Scene 6

Lights up on boat, we hear radio static. There is a heavy mist. On deck we see only black outline of Abuela with shawl over her head. We hear the Voices of Eduardo, Aída and Radio Operator.

EDUARDO'S VOICE. La Havana! Coming from San Pedro. Over.

RADIO OPERATOR'S VOICE. Right. DT6-6, you say you've lost a swimmer.

AÍDA'S VOICE. Our child, our only daughter . . . listen to me. Her name is Margarita Inez Suárez, she is wearing a black one-piece bathing suit cut high in the legs with a white racing stripe down the sides, a white bathing cap with goggles and her whole body covered with a . . . with a . . .

EDUARDO'S VOICE. With lanolin and paraffin.

AÍDA'S VOICE. *Sí . . . con* lanolin and paraffin. (*More radio static. Special on Simón, on the edge of the boat.*)

SIMÓN. Margo! Yo Margo! (*Pause*) Man don't do this. (*Pause.*) Come on. . . . Come on. . . . (*Pause.*) God, why does everything have to be so hard? (*Pause.*) Stupid. You know you're not supposed to die for this. Stupid. It's his dream and he can't even swim. (*Pause.*) Punch those arms in. Come home. Come home. I'm your little brother. Don't forget what Mama said. You're not supposed to leave me behind. *Vamos*, Margarita, take your little brother, hold his hand tight when you cross the street. He's so little. (*Pause.*) Oh Christ, give us a sign. . . . I know! I know! Margo, I'll send you a message . . . like mental telepathy. I'll hold my breath, close my eyes and I'll bring you home. (*He takes a deep breath; a few beats.*) This time I'll beep . . . I'll send out sonar signals like a dolphin. (*He imitates dolphin sounds. The sound of real dolphins takes over from Simón, then fades into sound of Abuela saying the Hail Mary in Spanish, as full lights come up slowly.*)

Scene 7

Eduardo coming out of cabin, sobbing, Aída holding him. Simón anxiously scanning the horizon. Abuela looking calmly ahead.

EDUARDO. *Es mi culpa, sí, es mi culpa.* (*He hits his chest.*)

AÍDA. *Ya, ya viejo* . . . it was my sin . . . I left my home.

EDUARDO. Forgive me, forgive me. I've lost our daughter, our sister, our granddaughter, *mi carne, mi sangre, mis ilu-*

46

siones. (*To heaven.*) *Dios mío* take me . . . take me, I say . . . Goddammit, take me!

SIMÓN. I'm going in.

AÍDA and EDUARDO. No!

EDUARDO. (*Grabbing and holding Simón, speaking to heaven.*) God, take me, not my children. They are my dreams, my illusions . . . and not this one, this one is my mystery . . . he has my secret dreams. In him are the parts of me I cannot see. (*Eduardo embraces Simón. Radio static becomes louder.*)

AÍDA. I . . . I think I see her.

SIMÓN. No it's just a seal.

ABUELA. (*Looking out with binoculars.*) *Mi nietacita, dónde estás?* (*She feels her heart.*) I don't feel the knife in my heart . . . my little fish is not lost. (*Radio crackles with static. As lights dim on boat, voices of Mel and Mary Beth are heard over the radio.*)

MEL'S VOICE. Tragedy has marred the face of the Wrigley Invitational Women's Race to Catalina. The Cuban swimmer, little Margarita Suárez, has reportedly been lost at sea. Coast Guard and divers are looking for her as we speak. Yet in spite of this tragedy the race must go on because . . .

MARY BETH'S VOICE. (*Interrupting loudly.*) Mel!

MEL'S VOICE. (*Startled.*) What!

MARY BETH'S VOICE. Ah . . . excuse me, Mel . . . we have a winner. We've just received word from Catalina that one of the swimmers is just fifty yards from the breakers . . . it's oh, it's Margarita Suárez! (*Special on family in cabin listening to radio.*)

MEL'S VOICE. What? I thought she died! (*Special on Margarita, taking off bathing cap, trophy in hand, walking on the water.*)

MARY BETH'S VOICE. Ahh . . . unless . . . unless this is a tragic. . . . No . . . there she is, Mel. Margarita Suárez! The only one in the race wearing a black bathing suit cut high in the legs with a racing stripe down the side. (*Family cheering, embracing.*)

SIMÓN. (*Screaming.*) Way to go Margo!

MEL'S VOICE. This is indeed a miracle! It's a resurrection!

47

Margarita Suárez with a flotilla of boats to meet her, is now walking on the waters, through the breakers . . . onto the beach, with crowds of people cheering her on. What a jubilation! This is a miracle! (*Sound of crowds cheering. Pinspot on Abuela.*)

ABUELA. *Sangre de mi sangre* you will be another to save us, ... to say to the evil one, *Coño Diablo, aqui estoy si me quieres.* (*Lights and cheering fade. Blackout.*)

END OF PLAY

PROPERTY LIST

Scene 2

Boat
Megaphone
Binoculars
Whistle
Radio

Scene 3

Timer

Scene 5

Training bottle
Net

Scene 7

Trophy

NEW PLAYS

★ **YELLOW FACE by David Henry Hwang.** Asian-American playwright DHH leads a protest against the casting of Jonathan Pryce as the Eurasian pimp in the original Broadway production of *Miss Saigon*, condemning the practice as "yellowface." The lines between truth and fiction blur with hilarious and moving results in this unreliable memoir. "A pungent play of ideas with a big heart." *–Variety.* "Fabulously inventive." *–The New Yorker.* [5M, 2W] ISBN: 978-0-8222-2301-6

★ **33 VARIATIONS by Moisés Kaufmann.** A mother coming to terms with her daughter. A composer coming to terms with his genius. And, even though they're separated by 200 years, these two people share an obsession that might, even just for a moment, make time stand still. "A compellingly original and thoroughly watchable play for today." *–Talkin' Broadway.* [4M, 4W] ISBN: 978-0-8222-2392-4

★ **BOOM by Peter Sinn Nachtrieb.** A grad student's online personal ad lures a mysterious journalism student to his subterranean research lab. But when a major catastrophic event strikes the planet, their date takes on evolutionary significance and the fate of humanity hangs in the balance. "Darkly funny dialogue." *–NY Times.* "Literate, coarse, thoughtful, sweet, scabrously inappropriate." *–Washington City Paper.* [1M, 2W] ISBN: 978-0-8222-2370-2

★ **LOVE, LOSS AND WHAT I WORE by Nora Ephron and Delia Ephron, based on the book by Ilene Beckerman.** A play of monologues and ensemble pieces about women, clothes and memory covering all the important subjects—mothers, prom dresses, mothers, buying bras, mothers, hating purses and why we only wear black. "Funny, compelling." *–NY Times.* "So funny and so powerful." *–WowOwow.com.* [5W] ISBN: 978-0-8222-2355-9

★ **CIRCLE MIRROR TRANSFORMATION by Annie Baker.** When four lost New Englanders enrolled in Marty's community center drama class experiment with harmless games, hearts are quietly torn apart, and tiny wars of epic proportions are waged and won. "Absorbing, unblinking and sharply funny." *–NY Times.* [2M, 3W] ISBN: 978-0-8222-2445-7

★ **BROKE-OLOGY by Nathan Louis Jackson.** The King family has weathered the hardships of life and survived with their love for each other intact. But when two brothers are called home to take care of their father, they find themselves strangely at odds. "Engaging dialogue." *–TheaterMania.com.* "Assured, bighearted." *–Time Out.* [3M, 1W] ISBN: 978-0-8222-2428-0

DRAMATISTS PLAY SERVICE, INC.
440 Park Avenue South, New York, NY 10016 212-683-8960 Fax 212-213-1539
postmaster@dramatists.com www.dramatists.com

NEW PLAYS

★ **A CIVIL WAR CHRISTMAS: AN AMERICAN MUSICAL CELEBRA-TION by Paula Vogel, music by Daryl Waters.** It's 1864, and Washington, D.C. is settling down to the coldest Christmas Eve in years. Intertwining many lives, this musical shows us that the gladness of one's heart is the best gift of all. "Boldly inventive theater, warm and affecting." *–Talkin' Broadway.* "Crisp strokes of dialogue." *–NY Times.* [12M, 5W] ISBN: 978-0-8222-2361-0

★ **SPEECH & DEBATE by Stephen Karam.** Three teenage misfits in Salem, Oregon discover they are linked by a sex scandal that's rocked their town. "Savvy comedy." *–Variety.* "Hilarious, cliché-free, and immensely entertaining." *–NY Times.* "A strong, rangy play." *–NY Newsday.* [2M, 2W] ISBN: 978-0-8222-2286-6

★ **DIVIDING THE ESTATE by Horton Foote.** Matriarch Stella Gordon is determined not to divide her 100-year-old Texas estate, despite her family's declining wealth and the looming financial crisis. But her three children have another plan. "Goes for laughs and succeeds." *–NY Daily News.* "The theatrical equivalent of a page-turner." *–Bloomberg.com.* [4M, 9W] ISBN: 978-0-8222-2398-6

★ **WHY TORTURE IS WRONG, AND THE PEOPLE WHO LOVE THEM by Christopher Durang.** Christopher Durang turns political humor upside down with this raucous and provocative satire about America's growing homeland "insecurity." "A smashing new play." *–NY Observer.* "You may laugh yourself silly." *–Bloomberg News.* [4M, 3W] ISBN: 978-0-8222-2401-3

★ **FIFTY WORDS by Michael Weller.** While their nine-year-old son is away for the night on his first sleepover, Adam and Jan have an evening alone together, beginning a suspenseful nightlong roller-coaster ride of revelation, rancor, passion and humor. "Mr. Weller is a bold and productive dramatist." *–NY Times.* [1M, 1W] ISBN: 978-0-8222-2348-1

★ **BECKY'S NEW CAR by Steven Dietz.** Becky Foster is caught in middle age, middle management and in a middling marriage—with no prospects for change on the horizon. Then one night a socially inept and grief-struck millionaire stumbles into the car dealership where Becky works. "Gently and consistently funny." *–Variety.* "Perfect blend of hilarious comedy and substantial weight." *–Broadway Hour.* [4M, 3W] ISBN: 978-0-8222-2393-1

DRAMATISTS PLAY SERVICE, INC.
440 Park Avenue South, New York, NY 10016 212-683-8960 Fax 212-213-1539
postmaster@dramatists.com www.dramatists.com

NEW PLAYS

★ **AT HOME AT THE ZOO by Edward Albee.** Edward Albee delves deeper into his play THE ZOO STORY by adding a first act, HOMELIFE, which precedes Peter's fateful meeting with Jerry on a park bench in Central Park. "An essential and heartening experience." –*NY Times.* "Darkly comic and thrilling." –*Time Out.* "Genuinely fascinating." –*Journal News.* [2M, 1W] ISBN: 978-0-8222-2317-7

★ **PASSING STRANGE book and lyrics by Stew, music by Stew and Heidi Rodewald, created in collaboration with Annie Dorsen.** A daring musical about a young bohemian that takes you from black middle-class America to Amsterdam, Berlin and beyond on a journey towards personal and artistic authenticity. "Fresh, exuberant, bracingly inventive, bitingly funny, and full of heart." –*NY Times.* "The freshest musical in town!" –*Wall Street Journal.* "Excellent songs and a vulnerable heart." –*Variety.* [4M, 3W] ISBN: 978-0-8222-2400-6

★ **REASONS TO BE PRETTY by Neil LaBute.** Greg really, truly adores his girlfriend, Steph. Unfortunately, he also thinks she has a few physical imperfections, and when he mentions them, all hell breaks loose. "Tight, tense and emotionally true." –*Time Magazine.* "Lively and compulsively watchable." –*The Record.* [2M, 2W] ISBN: 978-0-8222-2394-8

★ **OPUS by Michael Hollinger.** With only a few days to rehearse a grueling Beethoven masterpiece, a world-class string quartet struggles to prepare their highest-profile performance ever—a televised ceremony at the White House. "Intimate, intense and profoundly moving." –*Time Out.* "Worthy of scores of bravissimos." –*BroadwayWorld.com.* [4M, 1W] ISBN: 978-0-8222-2363-4

★ **BECKY SHAW by Gina Gionfriddo.** When an evening calculated to bring happiness takes a dark turn, crisis and comedy ensue in this wickedly funny play that asks what we owe the people we love and the strangers who land on our doorstep. "As engrossing as it is ferociously funny." –*NY Times.* "Gionfriddo is some kind of genius." –*Variety.* [2M, 3W] ISBN: 978-0-8222-2402-0

★ **KICKING A DEAD HORSE by Sam Shepard.** Hobart Struther's horse has just dropped dead. In an eighty-minute monologue, he discusses what path brought him here in the first place, the fate of his marriage, his career, politics and eventually the nature of the universe. "Deeply instinctual and intuitive." –*NY Times.* "The brilliance is in the infinite reverberations Shepard extracts from his simple metaphor." –*TheaterMania.* [1M, 1W] ISBN: 978-0-8222-2336-8

DRAMATISTS PLAY SERVICE, INC.
440 Park Avenue South, New York, NY 10016 212-683-8960 Fax 212-213-1539
postmaster@dramatists.com   www.dramatists.com